KU-344-720

Talking about Jesus

our call to everyday evangelisation

Jim McManus C.Ss.R.
and Bill Horton

Published by Redemptorist Publications
Wolf's Lane, Chawton, Hampshire, GU34 3HQ, UK
Tel. +44 (0)1420 88222, Fax. +44 (0)1420 88805
Email rp@rpbooks.co.uk, www.rpbooks.co.uk

A registered charity limited by guarantee.
Registered in England 03261721

First published March 2020

Text by Jim McManus and Bill Horton
Edited by Gráinne Treanor
Designed by Eliana Thompson

ISBN 978-0-85231-567-5

All rights reserved. No part of this publication may be reproduced, stored in a
retrieval system, or transmitted in any form or by any means, electronic, mechanical,
photocopying, recording or otherwise, without prior permission in writing from
Redemptorist Publications.

Copyright © Jim McManus and Bill Horton, 2020

The moral right of Jim McManus and Bill Horton to be identified as the authors of this
work has been asserted in accordance with the Copyright, Designs and Patents Act 1988.

A CIP catalogue record for this book is available from the British Library.

Every effort has been made to trace copyright holders and to obtain their permission
for the use of copyright material. The publisher apologises for any errors or omissions
and would be grateful for notification of any corrections that should be incorporated
in future reprints or editions of this book.

The publisher gratefully acknowledges permission to use the following copyright
material:
Excerpts from the New Revised Standard Version of the Bible: Anglicised Edition,
© 1989, 1995, Division of Christian Education of the National Council of the Churches
of Christ in the United States of America. Used by permission. All rights reserved.

Printed by John Dollin Printing Services Ltd.,
Whitchurch, Hants., RG28 7BB

Introduction

Jesus Christ has enormous confidence in us. He knows all our weaknesses and sinfulness and yet he commits his Gospel to us and asks us to make him known throughout the whole world. The great miracle is that Christian men and women have overcome all kinds of obstacles, including violent persecutions, down through the centuries. They have talked to others about their faith in Jesus Christ, and millions have responded gratefully and become Christians.

It is our turn now to talk about Jesus to the women and men of our time. We need to break the silence about the hope we have in our hearts because of our faith in Jesus Christ. Today we are his witnesses in the world.

The Lord has much more confidence in us than we have in ourselves. Many of us – perhaps most of us – feel that others are much better at making Christ known. We may feel inarticulate when it comes to talking to others about Jesus Christ and about our own faith in him. Perhaps we can talk eloquently about everything else, but when it comes to sharing our faith with others – telling others why we believe in our Saviour, Jesus Christ – we go silent. We need to break that silence. We know deep down in our hearts that we would love to make Christ known to others, especially to those who feel rejected by their society and who are looking for meaning and purpose in their lives.

That yearning to be able to make Christ known comes from the Holy Spirit. If you have that yearning in your heart and are willing to respond to the promptings of the Holy Spirit, you are halfway to becoming a good evangelist of the Lord.

The purpose of this short book is to help you to take the next step and begin to talk about Jesus. St Peter encourages us with these words: "Always be ready to make your defence to anyone who demands from you an account of the hope that is in you; yet do it with gentleness and reverence" (1 Peter

3:15-16). When someone asks you about how you are able to cope with disappointments and frustrations, with the death of loved ones or with your own sickness or disabilities and yet remain serene, you will be free to tell them that your faith in Christ gives you confidence and hope for your life in all circumstances.

In the first chapter we will look at how the first disciples were prepared by the Lord for their mission of making him known throughout the Roman Empire. We will see that Jesus prepared them by sending the Holy Spirit upon them. He prepares us today by sending that same Holy Spirit upon us.

In the second chapter we will look again at the message of salvation that those first disciples proclaimed all over the Roman Empire. We call this first proclamation of what Jesus did for us the *kerygma*. We want to share that message of salvation – the *kerygma* – with our own contemporaries, and we will need the help and inspiration of the Holy Spirit to do this.

In the third chapter we will look at ourselves, the messengers the Lord sends to bring the good news of his salvation to others. We will reflect on the parish community, which includes the school community, and on how the Lord is urging us to begin a new wave of evangelisation today. We are living in a very special time – the *kairos* time[1] – the time of salvation for the people of the twenty-first century. The Lord is asking us, his missionary disciples, to make him known to the peoples of our times. We hope this book encourages you to become active as the missionary disciple the Lord calls you to be.

At the end of each chapter you will find a brief introduction to a method of being still in God's presence. God says to us, "Be still, and know that I am God!" (Psalm 46:10). We encourage you to sit in stillness for ten to fifteen minutes and open your heart to receive God's gift of the Holy Spirit.

---

1   The term *kairos* comes from Greek and signifies a time of opportunity, decision or action.

CHAPTER 1

You will be my witnesses

Jesus told his disciples that they would be empowered by the Holy Spirit to be his witnesses. They would not have to depend on their own skills or learning. Just before he was taken up to heaven, he made them this promise:

> "But you will receive power when the Holy Spirit has come upon you; and you will be my witnesses in Jerusalem, in all Judea and Samaria, and to the ends of the earth." When he had said this, as they were watching, he was lifted up, and a cloud took him out of their sight (Acts 1:8-9).

Jesus was leaving them to the care and guidance of the Paraclete, the Holy Spirit. He promised them that the Holy Spirit would empower them to be his witnesses and that through this empowerment they would proclaim to the ends of the earth all that Jesus had done to secure the salvation of humanity. Those men and women didn't undertake this work of evangelisation through their own power. Jesus, as we read in the Acts of the Apostles, "ordered them not to leave Jerusalem, but to wait there for the promise of the Father" (Acts 1:4). They stayed in Jerusalem as they awaited the fulfilment of the Lord's promise.

The Holy Spirit came upon them at Pentecost, and St Luke describes what happened:

> When the day of Pentecost had come, they were all together in one place. And suddenly from heaven there came a sound like the rush of a violent wind, and it filled the entire house where they were sitting. Divided tongues, as of fire, appeared among them, and a tongue rested on each of them. All of them were filled with the Holy Spirit and began to speak in other languages, as the Spirit gave them ability (Acts 2:1-4).

The transformation of the frightened apostles

The apostles and other disciples had lived in fear after the death of Jesus. Now, through the empowerment of the Holy Spirit, they fearlessly went out onto the streets of Jerusalem and began preaching the good news that Jesus Christ, risen from the dead, was the promised Messiah and the Saviour of humanity. They proclaimed that the Christ who had been crucified had been raised by God to a new and eternal life for our salvation. They emphasised that the risen Lord Jesus had commissioned them through the Holy Spirit to bring this wonderful news to the very ends of the earth. St Luke records that on the day the Spirit first came upon them, "about three thousand persons were added" (Acts 2:41). Pentecost was truly the birthday of the Church. The Second Vatican Council clearly teaches: "Rising from the dead, [Jesus] sent His life-giving Spirit upon His disciples and through Him has established His Body which is the Church as the universal sacrament of salvation."[1]

Empowered by the Holy Spirit, the disciples of Jesus began their amazing mission of proclaiming Christ throughout the Roman Empire. The proclamation of Jesus Christ's resurrection from the dead for our salvation had begun. The Church of Christ became visible. Those first disciples of Jesus, empowered by the Holy Spirit, brought the good news of the salvation of humanity wherever they went.

The Holy Spirit is our teacher

We receive the same empowerment of the Holy Spirit. Jesus tells us that the Holy Spirit will be our teacher: "the Holy Spirit, whom the Father will send in my name, will teach you everything, and remind you of all that I have

---

1   Second Vatican Council, *Lumen Gentium* (Dogmatic Constitution on the Church), 48. Documents of the Church quoted throughout this book are available on the official website of the Holy See, www.vatican.va.

said to you" (John 14:26). Those first disciples of Jesus were fishermen, not theologians. When the Holy Spirit came upon them, they were filled with wisdom and qualified by the Spirit to proclaim the Gospel of Christ. We have that same Holy Spirit with us today as teacher and guide. As we invite God's Spirit into our hearts each day, opening our hearts to receive the gifts of the Holy Spirit, we are qualified to proclaim the Gospel of Christ. Jesus reminds us that when we doubt our ability to talk about Jesus, the Holy Spirit will be our teacher. We never go out on our own to talk about Jesus or to evangelise in his name. The Holy Spirit is always with us. Instead of saying, "I can't do it", we can say, "Come, Holy Spirit, and in your power I will do it." And the Holy Spirit will come afresh and give us the words to speak. Our trust is not in our own abilities or eloquence but in the power of the Holy Spirit.

The miracle of the Church

Guided and empowered by the Holy Spirit, the early disciples of Jesus went forth in confidence and began the great missionary work of making disciples of all nations. From a purely human point of view their task seemed impossible. The mighty Roman Empire, with all its gods, stood against them. Yet within thirty to forty years Christian communities had been established all over the Roman Empire. The evangelisation of that empire was not impossible for God, and the Church has continued to grow and spread all over the world, overcoming many bitter persecutions. Trusting in Christ's promise, the early disciples allowed themselves to be guided and taught by the Holy Spirit. They accomplished the mission that Christ their Lord had entrusted to them in the first century.

Pope St John Paul II's missionary vision

The Lord has entrusted the same mission to us in the twenty-first century. He depends on us to bring his Gospel, the good news of our salvation, to people in our society today. He is offering us the same support and guidance of the Holy Spirit. Many laymen and laywomen are now joyfully and wholeheartedly committed to the call of Christ to go and make disciples. In his great encyclical *Redemptoris Missio* ("Mission of the Reedemer"), Pope St John Paul II was able to write:

> The commitment of the laity to the work of evangelization is changing ecclesial life... Above all, there is a new awareness that *missionary activity is a matter for all Christians*, for all dioceses and parishes, Church institutions and associations.[2]

Are you aware of that commitment to evangelisation in your own local church, parish or diocese? Have you ever discussed this with a friend? You may be the person your parish has been waiting for to begin a new phase of evangelising your neighbourhood, town or city. The Holy Spirit will give you all the help you need.

Pope St John Paul II gave us a method for assessing the quality of our own local church. He wrote: "The effectiveness of the Church's organizations, movements, parishes and apostolic works must be measured in the light of this missionary imperative."[3]

Your parish is engaged in many different kinds of spiritual and social good works. If it is not actively involved in evangelisation, it will fail Pope St John Paul II's test. How would you rate your parish's missionary commitment? Perhaps you and a few other members of your parish are the ones God has chosen to make a new start. Would you be able to get a small group of committed parishioners together to

---

2   Pope St John Paul II, *Redemptoris Missio* ("Mission of the Reedemer"), 2.
3   Pope St John Paul II, *Redemptoris Missio*, 49.

explore a new missionary project? If you are in school, would you be willing to get a few like-minded students to become active evangelists?

Pope St John Paul II issued this urgent and challenging call-up to all our local churches: "No Christian community is faithful to its duty unless it is missionary: either it is a *missionary community* or it is not even a *Christian community*".[4]

On a scale of one to ten, where do you think your parish finds itself in Pope St John Paul II's vision of being a missionary community? Are you happy with that mark? Remember that you have the calling from God and the power to change it. You can make a new start. With the help of a few like-minded friends you can change the face of your parish. Your parish can become a missionary parish. Remember that the Holy Spirit has all the power, skill and wisdom necessary for every disciple to become a missionary disciple.

Pope Francis

Pope St John Paul II's vision of your local church being a missionary church is the major focus of Pope Francis' great apostolic exhortation, *Evangelii Gaudium* ("The Joy of the Gospel"):

> All the baptized, whatever their position in the Church or their level of instruction in the faith, are agents of evangelization, and it would be insufficient to envisage a plan of evangelization to be carried out by professionals while the rest of the faithful would simply be passive recipients. The new evangelization calls for personal involvement on the part of each of the baptized... we no longer say that we are "disciples" and "missionaries", but rather that we are always "missionary disciples".[5]

---

4   Pope St John Paul II, *Message of His Holiness Pope John Paul II for the World Mission Day 1991*, 1.
5   Pope Francis, *Evangelii Gaudium* ("The Joy of the Gospel"), 120.

Notice that Pope Francis is not restricting the work of evangelisation to those who are professionally trained. Each baptised person has a mission given to him or her by Christ to bring the good news of our salvation to others. Everyone who believes in Jesus Christ as their Saviour can talk about him to someone else. And, of course, we don't have to use many words. It is our way of living, our friendliness towards others and our concern for those who experience marginalisation in our society that proclaim Christ. As Pope St Paul VI said (including in his words a reference to his earlier *Address to the Members of the Consilium de Laicis* on 2 October 1974):

> [F]or the Church, the first means of evangelization is the witness of an authentically Christian life, given over to God in a communion that nothing should destroy and at the same time given to one's neighbor with limitless zeal... "Modern [people listen] more willingly to witnesses than to teachers, and if [they do listen] to teachers, it is because they are witnesses."[6]

You probably know parishioners – women and men full of faith and inner peace – who meet Pope St Paul VI's standard of witnessing. They have a word of encouragement for everyone and have become the great witnesses to Christ in your local church. Pope Benedict XVI describes them well when he writes: "We become witnesses when, through our actions, words and way of being, Another makes himself present."[7] Christ becomes present to others when these faithful parishioners, who are missionary disciples, are present. Verbally they may say very little, but non-verbally their whole life proclaims the Lord.

---

6   Pope St Paul VI, *Evangelii Nuntiandi* ("Evangelization in the Modern World"), 41.
7   Pope Benedict XVI, *Sacramentum Caritatis* ("The Sacrament of Charity"), 85.

The deepest identity of the Church

When you look at the world today and at the Church with its decreasing number of priests and religious sisters and brothers, we are sure you recognise that the work of evangelisation in the future will have to be carried on by our lay missionary disciples. In a prophetic moment Pope St John Paul II wrote that "God is opening before the Church the horizons of a humanity more fully prepared for the sowing of the Gospel. I sense that the moment has come to commit all of the Church's energies to a new evangelization".[8]

John Paul, as well as being a great saint and scholar, was a practical man, with his two feet firmly on the ground. His vision of the commitment of the laity to the work of the new evangelisation is now being shared by hundreds of thousands of our committed laity throughout the Church. If you don't see signs of this commitment in your own parish, don't despair. And don't give in to the temptation to believe that you are not capable. Christ's first disciples hid away from the people of Jerusalem until the Holy Spirit came upon them and gave them the courage to go out and proclaim the good news of Jesus Christ. That same Holy Spirit is with you and with all your parishioners and friends. The Holy Spirit wants you to joyfully live the true identity of the Church. This is Pope St Paul VI's great teaching:

> Evangelizing is in fact the grace and vocation proper to the Church, her deepest identity. She exists in order to evangelize, that is to say, in order to preach and teach, to be the channel of the gift of grace, to reconcile sinners with God, and to perpetuate Christ's sacrifice in the Mass, which is the memorial of His death and glorious resurrection.[9]

---

8   Pope St John Paul II, *Redemptoris Missio*, 3.
9   Pope St Paul VI, *Evangelii Nuntiandi*, 14.

The Church doesn't exist just for her own members. The Church exists for those who have not yet heard the good news of their salvation in Jesus Christ. With Pope Francis we say that the Church must remain "permanently in a state of mission".[10] This mission will not be completed until Christ comes again. Each of us is engaged in the mission of the Church. And if we are not yet engaged in that mission, we are depriving ourselves of "the joy of the Gospel". Nothing will give you greater joy than to introduce another person to Jesus Christ.

The gentle action of the Spirit

We can learn a great deal from those men and women who have been actively involved in the work of the new evangelisation for some years. Many dioceses have developed good training programmes and discovered techniques that work for them. It is prudent to learn from their experience. At the same time, we remind ourselves of what Pope St Paul VI, the father of the new evangelisation, wrote:

> Techniques of evangelization are good, but even the most advanced ones could not replace the gentle action of the Spirit. The most perfect preparation of the evangelizer has no effect without the Holy Spirit. Without the Holy Spirit the most convincing dialectic has no power over the heart of [humankind]. Without Him the most highly developed schemas resting on a sociological or psychological basis are quickly seen to be quite valueless.[11]

---

10 Pope Francis, *Evangelii Gaudium*, 25 (quoting from the Fifth General Conference of the Latin American and Caribbean Bishops, *Aparecida Document*, 29 June 2007, 551).
11 Pope St Paul VI, *Evangelii Nuntiandi*, 75.

When we open our hearts to the Holy Spirit, we are empowered to proclaim all that Christ has done for us and for the whole human race. In taking up our mission from Christ to make disciples of our generation we are collaborators with the Holy Spirit. The Holy Spirit alone can empower us to talk about what Jesus has done for us in a way that makes sense to the people we are talking to. That is Jesus' promise to us. Our first step in becoming evangelists, then, is to invoke the Holy Spirit to come upon us afresh. Listen to what Pope St Paul VI said:

> Evangelization will never be possible without the action of the Holy Spirit... It is the Holy Spirit who, today just as at the beginning of the Church, acts in every evangelizer who allows himself [or herself] to be possessed and led by Him. The Holy Spirit places on his [or her] lips the words which he [or she] could not find by [him- or herself], and at the same time the Holy Spirit predisposes the soul of the hearer to be open and receptive to the Good News and to the kingdom being proclaimed.[12]

Without the power of the Holy Spirit none of us can speak about Jesus Christ in a way that touches the hearts of others. It is the Holy Spirit who gives us the words to speak when we seek to proclaim what Jesus has done for us. And it is the Holy Spirit who opens the hearts of our listeners to hear God's word and accept Jesus as their Saviour. When we keep this full awareness of God's Spirit at work in the hearts of our listeners and in our own hearts, we can confidently speak about Our Lord Jesus Christ. We will fulfil our mission as missionary disciples and make Christ known to others.

---

12 Pope St Paul VI, *Evangelii Nuntiandi*, 75.

A company of evangelists

The lone evangelist will struggle without the support of others, and many will give up. Every parish is in urgent need of an association of lay evangelists: women and men committed to Christ and to supporting one another in the joyful but challenging mission of making Jesus Christ known to others. If you feel within you a commitment to the new evangelisation so vital for the survival and renewal of the Church today, talk to other committed missionary disciples in your parish or neighbourhood and form an association. Your parish will then be doing what Pope Francis expects every parish to do when he writes that in all its activities "the parish encourages and trains its members to be evangelizers".[13]

The Holy Spirit will guide you as you discuss with like-minded missionary disciples the need to form an association of lay evangelists for the growth and, in places, the very survival of the Church. Jesus is saying to you and your friends, "you will be my witnesses" (Acts 1:8). Your response to this invitation is a big thank you to the Lord for the trust he has in you and a reminder to him that you will depend totally on the power of the Holy Spirit. And, for yourself and those to whom the Lord is sending you, say a prayer to the Holy Spirit each day.

---

13 Pope Francis, *Evangelii Gaudium*, 28.

Personal spiritual exercise

Begin with this official prayer of the Church to the Holy Spirit.

Come, Holy Spirit, fill the hearts of your faithful and enkindle in them the fire of your love. Send forth your Spirit and they shall be created. And you shall renew the face of the earth.

O God, who by the light of the Holy Spirit did instruct the hearts of the faithful, grant that by the same Holy Spirit we may be truly wise and ever enjoy his consolations. Through Christ Our Lord. Amen.

Take some time now (ten to fifteen minutes) to be still in God's presence and open your heart to receive the gift of the Holy Spirit.

- Centre yourself; sit upright, two feet firmly on the floor; breathe rhythmically with deep breaths, in and out, from the abdomen; clear your mind of all preoccupations.

- Bring yourself to bodily stillness.

- Now hear in your heart the great promise of Jesus: "you will receive power when the Holy Spirit has come upon you; and you will be my witnesses in Jerusalem, in all Judea and Samaria, and to the ends of the earth" (Acts 1:8).

- Quietly repeat this great promise.

- Thank the Father for this gift of the power of the Holy Spirit that empowers you to witness to Christ.

- You may find it helpful if you name to God a specific area of weakness or sin in your life where you need healing and forgiveness.

- Now be still for some time in the presence of God as you welcome the Holy Spirit into your heart.

- As you are about to finish your time of prayer, focus again on your breathing while you relax in God's presence.

- Bring yourself gently back to your daily concerns.

This spiritual exercise will deepen your awareness of the presence of the Holy Spirit in your heart and give you confidence that the Spirit will be with you in everything you do to make Christ known.

CHAPTER 2

The message of salvation

The first announcement of our salvation through the death and resurrection of Jesus Christ was called, in the early Church, the *kerygma* – a Greek word that means a public proclamation. It was the proclamation of the person of our Lord Jesus Christ risen from the dead. Christ was at the centre of each proclamation of salvation. The proclamation of the Gospel is about what Christ has done for us, through his death and resurrection, to secure our salvation. It is not about what we must do to merit our salvation. Salvation is always a free gift of God. Jesus told Nicodemus, who came to see him at night, that our salvation is entirely the gift of God:

> For God so loved the world that he gave his only Son, so that everyone who believes in him may not perish but may have eternal life. Indeed, God did not send the Son into the world to condemn the world, but in order that the world might be saved through him (John 3:16-17).

A compelling message

Our proclamation of God's desire for all people to be saved is a compelling message, especially for those who are searching for meaning and purpose in life, and most of all for those who are seeking that inner transformation that the Holy Spirit alone can effect in the human heart through the grace of God. People who have been hurt deeply by the sins of others against them or by their own sins and who are yearning for a fresh start and a clean heart find comfort in this great promise of God:

> I will sprinkle clean water upon you, and you shall be clean from all your uncleannesses, and from all your idols I will cleanse you. A new heart I will give you, and a new spirit I will put within you; and I will remove from your body the heart of stone and give you a heart of flesh. I will put my spirit within you (Ezekiel 36:25-27).

That divine promise speaks directly to the yearning of the human heart for wholeness. Those who are sincerely seeking a new and grace-filled life gain great encouragement through it. This great promise of God the Father is fulfilled through Jesus Christ, who says, "The thief comes only to steal and kill and destroy. I came that they may have life, and have it abundantly" (John 10:10).

Life in abundance is the gift that Jesus Christ gives to us poor sinners. No matter how immoral people may have been, they are filled with grace once they turn to Christ for help and accept him as their Saviour. Their sins are forgiven, their hearts are purified and they are filled with inner peace. St Paul says clearly:

> [I]f you confess with your lips that Jesus is Lord and believe in your heart that God raised him from the dead, you will be saved. For one believes with the heart and so is justified, and one confesses with the mouth and so is saved (Romans 10:9-10).

Jesus came to take away all our sins and give us life in abundance.

The abundant life

Christian life is a life full of love and inner peace. Without that love and peace, the human heart is full of turmoil. Seeking inner peace and joy in earthly possessions is pointless. What fills your bank account or your garage can't fulfil your heart's yearning for the abundant life. The human heart – the very core of the human being – is spiritual, and only the spiritual can fulfil its yearning. No pleasures or material riches can impart peace and serenity to the human heart. St Augustine's famous words are as true today as they were sixteen hundred years ago: "you have made us for yourself, and our heart is restless until it rests in you".[1] Augustine ultimately found the rest he sought when he opened his heart to Jesus Christ and welcomed him as his Lord and Saviour.

---

1   St Augustine, *Confessions*, 1.1, translated by Henry Chadwick (Oxford: Oxford University Press, 1991), 3.

The Gospel is called "the Good News" because it tells us about the abundant life that Jesus offers us and how we can receive it. That is what the new evangelisation is all about. We seek to bring to our brothers and sisters, who may have been searching in vain for inner peace, the knowledge of Jesus Christ who is our peace. If some troubled friend ever says to you, "I wish I could find a little peace", you can tell him or her that Jesus Christ came precisely to give us abundant peace. He said to his disciples at the Last Supper, "Peace I leave with you; my peace I give to you. I do not give to you as the world gives. Do not let your hearts be troubled, and do not let them be afraid" (John 14:27).

Jesus Christ offers his gift of peace to all who turn to him. That surely is good news. Of course, each person is quite entitled to ask us the question, "If you say Jesus Christ is so good, tell me, what has he ever done for you?" This question opens the door to a fruitful discussion about Jesus, especially if you can share one or two personal moments in your life when you really needed the Lord's help to get you through a difficult situation. If you can share with your friend how Jesus gave you peace in a time of trouble, you will be evangelising effectively. St Peter writes about this:

> Do not fear what they fear, and do not be intimidated, but in your hearts sanctify Christ as Lord. Always be ready to make your defence to anyone who demands from you an account of the hope that is in you; yet do it with gentleness and reverence (1 Peter 3:14-16).

You need that gentleness and reverence when you are seeking to introduce someone to Jesus Christ. You don't have all the answers to life's difficulties, but you have the most important one: Jesus Christ will walk with those who turn to him through all their difficulties and will give them peace.

Christr is our peace

Wᵉ can sum up the whole Gospel message of our salvation with those four words: Christ is our peace. Peace alone fulfils the human heart. People who have everything that this world can provide, but lack peace of heart, are very unhappy. The happy heart is full of love, joy and peace. These are spiritual gifts, and the heart that opens to God will receive them. The heart that is closed to God is closed to the spiritual world and cannot receive this love, joy and peace. Why are so many people in our world unhappy? It is because so often they are looking for happiness in all the wrong places.

Pope St John Paul II gives us the secret of happiness in this succinct phrase: "Happiness is being rooted in love".[2] Jesus' whole message is about love: about God's love for us in creating us; about Christ's love for us in redeeming us; and about the love we should have in our hearts for our neighbours whom, as Jesus says, we love as we love ourselves. Indeed, Jesus says we have love in our hearts even for our enemies: "But I say to you, Love your enemies and pray for those who persecute you, so that you may be children of your Father in heaven" (Matthew 5:44).

This love is given to us by the Holy Spirit who dwells in our hearts. St Paul wrote, "God's love has been poured into our hearts through the Holy Spirit that has been given to us" (Romans 5:5). When we think about evangelisation, we should always reflect again on the Holy Spirit, who makes us one with Christ and alive in Christ. Pope St John Paul II wrote:

> The present-day Church seems to repeat with ever greater fervour and with holy insistence: "Come, Holy Spirit!" Come! Come!... This appeal to the Spirit, intended precisely to obtain the Spirit, is the answer to all the "materialisms" of our age.[3]

---

2   Pope St John Paul II, *Man and Woman He Created Them: a theology of the body* (Boston, MA: Pauline Books and Media, 2006), 16:2.
3   Pope St John Paul II, *Redemptor Hominis* ("The Redeemer of Man"), 18.

No matter what difficulties we face in life, we have the answer. We can invoke the Holy Spirit. It is when we are trying to interest another person in Our Lord Jesus Christ that we should silently and confidently invoke the Holy Spirit to heal the hurt that may have been inflicted on the person by sin, even though the person may be unaware of this.

Disruption of sin

Sin is a failure to love, and it robs the conscience of peace. The *Catechism of the Catholic Church* provides a helpful definition of sin when it states:

> Sin is an offence against reason, truth and right conscience; it is failure in genuine love for God and neighbour caused by a perverse attachment to certain goods. It wounds the nature of [the person] and injures human solidarity.[4]

Sin uses others or abuses others; sin puts selfish self-satisfaction before everything else. Sin leads to the disintegration of peace, happiness and serenity. But Jesus Christ came to take away all our sins. St Paul proclaimed this good news: "Let it be known to you therefore... that through this man forgiveness of sins is proclaimed to you; by this Jesus everyone who believes is set free from all those sins" (Acts 13:38-39).

St Paul goes on to spell out to the Church in Corinth how God has done all this for us through Christ. He writes:

> [I]f anyone is in Christ, there is a new creation: everything old has passed away; see, everything has become new! All this is from God, who reconciled us to himself through Christ, and has given us the ministry of reconciliation (2 Corinthians 5:17-18).

---

4 *Catechism of the Catholic Church*, 1849. Quotations from the *Catechism of the Catholic Church* throughout this book are taken from the CTS Definitive and Complete Edition (London: Catholic Truth Society, 2016).

That surely is the good news that so many people today desperately want to hear. We can let go of all our past sins, no matter how grievous, because our sins are forgiven once we accept Jesus Christ as our Saviour.

When people hear today what Jesus Christ has done for them, their hearts will be touched, and they will want to know what they should do. St Luke tells us how the first converts to Christ in Jerusalem responded to St Peter's proclamation of what Jesus had done and how God had raised him from the dead after he had been crucified:

> [T]hey were cut to the heart and said to Peter and the other apostles, "Brothers, what should we do?" Peter said to them, "Repent, and be baptized every one of you in the name of Jesus Christ so that your sins may be forgiven; and you will receive the gift of the Holy Spirit" (Acts 2:37-38).

God's merciful and healing response to our sinfulness, once we are sorry and seek to change our direction in life, is forgiveness. We receive new life through the gift of the Holy Spirit. If you are talking with somebody who is searching for new life and they are curious about the Holy Spirit and forgiveness of sins, you might say to them, "The best way to understand this is in a short prayer." If the person is willing, lay your hand on his or her shoulder and say, "Come, Holy Spirit, and fill my brother or sister with the new life of Christ the Lord." Alternatively, say your own favourite prayer to the Holy Spirit.

You could repeat the prayer a few times and invite the person to join you in asking Jesus to pour out the Holy Spirit with all the gifts of salvation. Also, encourage the person to frequently invite the Holy Spirit into his or her heart. Normally, if people are sincerely seeking, they will begin to experience deep conversion. It is important, then, to keep in touch with them or to put them in touch with a few committed Christians.

The message of salvation

Christians have the message of salvation for the whole human race. We must deliver it with great gentleness and respect and with joy and confidence. The announcement of who Jesus Christ is and what he has done for us is the heart of the proclamation of the Gospel. The word that proclaims what Jesus does for us through his death and resurrection is not just a human word; it is also a word of God spoken by Jesus himself. Christ is present in that very act of proclaiming what he has done for us.

Centrality of the *kerygma*

We should never presume that the *kerygma* – the good news of what Jesus Christ has done for us – has been heard and assimilated. Many Catholics fit the category of having been baptised but not evangelised. They have never had an encounter with Christ or got to know him personally as their Lord and Saviour. Pope Benedict XVI expressed the essence of our Christian faith when he wrote, "Being Christian is not the result of an ethical choice or a lofty idea, but the encounter with an event, a person, which gives life a new horizon and a decisive direction."[5]

People's faith will be weak and remain at risk until they have that personal encounter with Christ through which they develop their own personal relationship with him. Pope Francis is very alert to this. He writes:

> The centrality of the *kerygma* calls for stressing those elements which are most needed today: it has to express God's saving love which precedes any moral and religious obligation on our part; it should not impose the truth but appeal to freedom; it should be marked by joy, encouragement, liveliness and a harmonious balance which will not reduce preaching to a few doctrines which are at times more philosophical than evangelical. All this demands on the part of the evangelizer

---

5   Pope Benedict XVI, *Deus Caritas Est* ("God is Love"), 1.

certain attitudes which foster openness to the message: approachability, readiness for dialogue, patience, a warmth and welcome which is non-judgmental.[6]

The challenge we are facing in our work of evangelisation today is twofold. First, many people who say they don't believe in God have never heard of Jesus Christ. Second, many who have heard of him think he is merely a great historical figure of the past. They have not yet heard the good news of the new life Jesus offers to us through his death and resurrection from the dead; they haven't heard that he is our Saviour who wants to take away all our sins; they haven't heard that he is the one who fills our whole being with the Holy Spirit; they haven't heard that he is the only one who can fill our hearts with the peace we crave for; they haven't heard that Jesus came to give us the abundant life that comes from God our Father; they haven't heard that God is their loving Father and that he dwells within them; they haven't heard the *kerygma* – the message of their salvation.

It is our mission today to proclaim this good news of all that Jesus has done for us. As St Paul wrote:

> God, who is rich in mercy, out of the great love with which he loved us even when we were dead through our trespasses, made us alive together with Christ – by grace you have been saved – and raised us up with him and seated us with him in the heavenly places in Christ Jesus, so that in the ages to come he might show the immeasurable riches of his grace in kindness towards us in Christ Jesus (Ephesians 2:4-7).

The Gospel of Jesus Christ which we proclaim is surely the best news people can hear about themselves in our world today. Our Church needs joyful and confident proclaimers of this life-giving good news in every parish, diocese and country. Will you do your best to respond and assemble a team of lay evangelists who will learn how to bring this good news of Our Lord Jesus Christ to those who have as yet never heard it?

---

6   Pope Francis, *Evangelii Gaudium*, 165.

Personal spiritual exercise

Begin with this prayer to the Holy Spirit.

Come, Holy Spirit, fill the hearts of your faithful and enkindle in them the fire of your love. Send forth your Spirit and they shall be created. And you shall renew the face of the earth.

O God, who by the light of the Holy Spirit did instruct the hearts of the faithful, grant that by the same Holy Spirit we may be truly wise and ever enjoy his consolations. Through Christ Our Lord. Amen.

Take some time now (ten to fifteen minutes) to be still in God's presence and open your heart to receive the gift of the Holy Spirit.

- Centre yourself; sit upright, two feet firmly on the floor; breathe rhythmically with deep breaths, in and out, from the abdomen; clear your mind of all preoccupations.

- Bring yourself to bodily stillness.

- Now welcome in your heart this gift that Jesus has for you: "Peace I leave with you; my peace I give to you. I do not give to you as the world gives. Do not let your hearts be troubled, and do not let them be afraid" (John 14:27).

- Quietly repeat those words of Jesus and hand over to him all worries or trouble.

- You may find it helpful if you name to God a specific area of weakness or sin in your life where you need healing and forgiveness.

- Now be still for some time in the presence of God as you welcome the Holy Spirit into your heart.

- As you are about to finish your time of prayer, focus again on your breathing while you relax in God's presence.

- Bring yourself gently back to your daily concerns.

This spiritual exercise will deepen your awareness of the presence of the Holy Spirit in your heart and give you confidence that the Spirit will be with you in everything you do to make Christ known.

CHAPTER 3

The messengers of Christ

We reflected in the last chapter on the message of salvation that Christ wants us to share with others. We will now reflect on ourselves, the messengers of Christ, asking how well prepared we are for delivering the message of salvation to others.

Each of us has received the gift of the Holy Spirit. We are qualified by the Spirit to share our faith with others and to spread the good news that Christ has redeemed us. The Holy Spirit wants us to share this good news by the way we live and seek to help others.

God's work

Each of us has been gifted by the Lord with the *charisms* of the Spirit that we need for our specific missionary work. St Paul wrote:

> [E]ach of us was given grace according to the measure of Christ's gift... to equip the saints for the work of ministry, for building up the body of Christ, until all of us come to the unity of the faith and of the knowledge of the Son of God, to maturity, to the measure of the full stature of Christ (Ephesians 4:7. 12-13).

Charisms are so called after the Greek term used by St Paul to signify a favour, gratuitous gift or benefit. They are described in the *Catechism of the Catholic Church* as *special graces*, among which are "the *graces of state* that accompany the exercise of the responsibilities of the Christian life and of the ministries within the Church".[1] They might be described as special talents given to us so that we can be empowered to fulfil our missionary work.

---

1 *Catechism of the Catholic Church*, 2004.

The guiding presence of the Holy Spirit is the great gift that God the Father gives us "to equip us" for our work as missionary disciples. The Second Vatican Council made it clear that the Church is established by Christ when the Spirit is poured out. *Lumen Gentium* states that "by communicating his Spirit, Christ mystically constitutes as his body his brothers and sisters who are called together from every nation."[2]

With the gift of the Holy Spirit we don't become an organisation called the Catholic Church; we become the mystical body of Christ in the world. We become one with Christ. He lives in us and our true Christian life is lived in him. Jesus says to us, "Abide in me as I abide in you. Just as the branch cannot bear fruit by itself unless it abides in the vine, neither can you unless you abide in me. I am the vine, you are the branches" (John 15:4-5).

The Church would be incapable of action without the Holy Spirit and the gifts of the Spirit. Getting to know the Holy Spirit is the spiritual quest in the heart of each believer in Christ. That is why Jesus assures us that the Father will always give the gift of the Spirit to those who ask him. He says to us, "If you then, who are evil, know how to give good gifts to your children, how much more will the heavenly Father give the Holy Spirit to those who ask him!" (Luke 11:13).

The Holy Spirit is our teacher

It is very helpful and indeed necessary for us to become aware daily of the abiding presence of the Holy Spirit at work in the Church, in the world, in our lives and in our hearts. The Spirit is the active memory of the Church, the teacher of our faith. The *Catechism of the Catholic Church* tells us that "by his transforming power, [the Holy Spirit] makes the mystery of Christ present here and now".[3] The Spirit is

---

2 Second Vatican Council, *Lumen Gentium*, 7, in Austin Flannery, O.P. (ed.), *Vatican Council II* (Dublin: Dominican Publications, 1996), 6.
3 *Catechism of the Catholic Church*, 1092.

witnessed in all the good works of Christians all over the world as they seek to live the life of Christ, and when we pray it is the Spirit who prays in our hearts. The Spirit prepares our minds and hearts for the work of evangelisation.

If you call upon the Holy Spirit in your prayer to come into your heart and mind, if you listen to the guidance of the Spirit and allow the Holy Spirit to lead you, you are equipped to undertake the work of sharing your faith in Christ with others. The more you share your faith with others, the more confident you will become and the more you will learn about evangelising. You will be taught by the Spirit. Remember the words of Jesus when he said that "the Holy Spirit, whom the Father will send in my name, will teach you everything, and remind you of all I have said to you" (John 14:26).

Witness is at the heart of evangelisation

Your witness to Christ becomes manifest in many ways: by your care and concern for others; by your respect for each person no matter how he or she behaves; by your readiness to go the extra mile to help a person in need; and, of course, by your willingness to share the good news of Jesus Christ. This is the witness that Christ has in mind when he says to us, "you will be my witnesses" (Acts 1:8). If many people in a parish are giving that kind of witness, others will be attracted to join them. They will have seen the face of Christ in the witness of the parishioners.

Pope Francis describes the parish in this way:

> The parish is the presence of the Church in a given territory, an environment for hearing God's word, for growth in the Christian life, for dialogue, proclamation, charitable outreach, worship and celebration. In all its activities the parish encourages and trains its members to be evangelizers.[4]

---

4   Pope Francis, *Evangelii Gaudium*, 28.

Notice that last sentence: "In all its activities the parish encourages and trains its members to be evangelizers." In the first chapter we suggested that Pope Francis expects every parish to train evangelisers. Your parish could do that if you and some other parishioners formed a lay association of evangelists.[5]

Nobody will be knocking on the door to join a parish community if the parish is not reaching out in love to everyone in the neighbourhood and if nothing about that parish community attracts the outsider. It is the attitude we have towards people that attracts them to us. Each of us can ask ourselves, "Am I a warm, welcoming person as I approach people, or do I emit signals of suspicion?" It is vital that we are in the right frame of mind as we approach people, because that first encounter with another person needs to communicate – both verbally and non-verbally (for example, in our body language) – our welcome, respect, acceptance and genuine love for and interest in this brother or sister. We need to see the encounter in itself as the beginning of evangelisation.

It is the Holy Spirit who teaches us how to relate in love to each person. Through our love, respect and acceptance of the person, "Another makes himself present".[6] Christ himself becomes present, and because Christ becomes present, the other person may experience the love and goodness of the Lord for the first time.

Listening

Our primary attitude as messengers of Christ is one of listening. The good evangelist is always a good listener. If the other person wants to talk about his or her life, we listen respectfully, accept the sincerity of his or her sharing,

---

5 You are probably wondering how these lay evangelists could be trained. We recommend the book *Sent to Proclaim the Gospel: honouring the legacy of St Paul VI* by Fr Jim McManus C.Ss.R. (Chawton: Redemptorist Publications, 2018). This book was written to help lay evangelists as they prepare for their work of evangelisation.
6 Pope Benedict XVI, *Sacramentum Caritatis*, 85.

and refrain from giving advice until we are asked for it. When the person asks us what he or she should do to experience peace of heart, we can gently share with him or her how our own faith in Jesus Christ helps us to live peacefully with our own personal struggles. The redemption that we know in our own lives doesn't make us immune to life's struggles and disappointments. But it gives us hope, peace and the guarantee that our sins are forgiven when we repent and open our hearts to receive God's Spirit. In the Creed of our Sunday Mass we confess our faith in the Holy Spirit in this way: "I believe in the Holy Spirit, the Lord, the giver of life".[7] That is the redemption that each person is searching for – new life in the Spirit.

An oasis of mercy

When a person in need of peace meets a loving, non-judgemental, joyful evangelist who is more interested in him or her as a person than in making a convert, that person has reached "an oasis of mercy" – a safe place where he or she feels acceptance and affirmation. The person knows that he or she will not be judged, rejected or condemned. On the need for this "oasis" Pope Francis wrote:

> [W]herever the Church is present, the mercy of the Father must be evident. In our parishes, communities, associations and movements, in a word, wherever there are Christians, everyone should find an oasis of mercy.[8]

There is goodness in every human being. God has put it there. The sensitive missionary disciple knows how to affirm this goodness in the other person. Interest in the person, expressed in empathetic listening and good conversation, will eventually lead to the question of identity, to how this person sees self, accepts self, loves self. At this stage a word of encouragement often releases a person's cry for meaning in life. For instance, the simple remark, "You're a good person

---

7   Nicene Creed.
8   Pope Francis, *Misericordiae Vultus* (Bull of the Extraordinary Year of Mercy), 12.

and you have done your best in difficult situations", may quickly get the response, "But I was very mean to my wife and now she is dead and I feel very guilty and nothing I do can get rid of the guilt." Now you have the cue for talking about salvation, about God's forgiveness, about the healing of inner wounds, about Christ who came specifically to take away all our sins and heal every wound in our hearts.

Notice the progression here. We begin with a word of encouragement; we acknowledge the person's goodness; we assure the person that he or she was trying to do his or her best. Individuals may accept most of that but then begin to talk about a time when they know they did wrong, violating sacred relationships, and are now feeling guilty and crying out for a saviour. They have moved from "I am all right the way I am" to "I need help right now because of the way I am." They acknowledge that they need a saviour who can heal their hearts and give a new meaning to their lives.

Patiently listening to individuals' stories, acknowledging their innate goodness, and accepting them just as they are opens the door to their hearts. Now they are willing to hear and accept the good news of their salvation in Christ.

Developing good attitudes

Missionary disciples must train themselves daily to listen attentively to those who may be showing some interest in faith, religion or Jesus Christ. We must purge our minds and hearts of all negativity. As missionary disciples we never engage in negative gossip about any person or any group. Negativity in the heart about anyone – and especially about those who may not respond to our efforts at evangelising – is a real poison in the spirit. It can, of course, be disappointing and even frustrating if we have worked hard trying to interest a group in the Lord and yet get no response. But that should never cause us to be negative or sarcastic about any person or group. Jesus himself experienced irresponsiveness from certain groups, especially in his home town of Nazareth, as recorded in the Gospel of Mark:

> On the sabbath he began to teach in the synagogue, and many who heard him were astounded... And they took offence at him... And he could do no deed of power there, except that he laid his hands on a few sick people and cured them. And he was amazed at their unbelief (Mark 6:2-3. 5-6).

We have the mind of Christ

Christ's missionary disciples today will also frequently be amazed at the lack of faith that some people show. But they never indulge in criticism or condemnation. They cultivate Christ's own attitudes. St Paul can say, "we have the mind of Christ" (1 Corinthians 2:16). If we think with "the mind of Christ" we will not go astray. But we must constantly learn from Christ as he invites us with the words, "Take my yoke upon you, and learn from me; for I am gentle and humble in heart, and you will find rest for your souls. For my yoke is easy, and my burden is light" (Matthew 11:29-30). As we cultivate this gentleness and humbleness of Christ, we will not feel obliged to win every argument or be praised for everything we try to do. St Paul encouraged the Philippians when he said:

> Let the same mind be in you that was in Christ Jesus, who, though he was in the form of God, did not regard equality with God as something to be exploited, but emptied himself, taking the form of a slave, being born in human likeness (Philippians 2:5-7).

When we seek to live with the mind of Christ we will be ready to calmly and lovingly reach out to everyone. We will not be disappointed when we get no response from others and we will take all our efforts to God in prayer.

Learning from Christ how to give time to prayer

We know that the attitudes we need to bring to our work as missionary disciples must be the same attitudes that Jesus had. We can only develop these attitudes by imitating Christ's prayer life. Jesus gave a lot of time to prayer. Sometimes he spent the whole night in prayer. If he, the Son of God, saw prayer as an essential component of his missionary life, we, his poor disciples, must also have prayer as a priority in our missionary lives. Jesus' first disciples carefully observed his every move and listened intently to every word he spoke. They knew that he gave a lot of time to prayer. St Luke is the evangelist who dwells most on Jesus at prayer. He writes that Jesus "was praying in a certain place, and after he had finished, one of his disciples said to him, 'Lord, teach us to pray, as John taught his disciples.' He said to them, 'When you pray, say: Father, hallowed be your name.'" (Luke 11:1-2)

On that occasion Jesus taught them his prayer – the Lord's Prayer, or the "Our Father" as we often call it. The disciples were now getting their first glimpse into how Jesus was praying. He was in the presence of his Father and he was having a loving conversation with his Father. That is how Jesus wanted his disciples to pray and it is how Jesus wants us to pray. We too are in the presence of our Father when we pray. Like Jesus, we too can be having a loving conversation with our God.

The Lord's Prayer is the great prayer of Christian people of all denominations. It forms within our spirits and hearts the awareness of who we truly are as sons and daughters of our heavenly Father. We should also be aware that in calling God our "Father" we are also including all the tenderness of God as "Mother". In the *Catechism of the Catholic Church* we read, "God's parental tenderness can also be expressed by the image of motherhood, which emphasises God's immanence, the intimacy between Creator and creature."[9]

---

9   *Catechism of the Catholic Church*, 239.

If the image of father doesn't speak to someone about the goodness and love of God, the image of mother may do so. There can be a wound in the heart – a "father wound" – a space left empty because of the absence of one's father, and the absence of a father's love, encouragement and compassion. But that wound in the heart of God's sons or daughters will be healed if they bring it into God's presence and allow themselves to be embraced by the motherly tenderness of God.

In the scriptures God compares Godself to a mother in this way: "As a mother comforts her child, so I will comfort you" (Isaiah 66:13). And in the Psalms we read, "I have calmed and quieted my soul, like a weaned child with its mother" (Psalm 131:2). Jesus calls us into an intimate, trusting, loving relationship with God.

The effectiveness of prayer

Jesus didn't send his disciples out empty-handed to make disciples. He shared with them his own secret – his relationship with God his Father and with the Holy Spirit. Jesus guarantees that when we ask the Father for the gift of the Holy Spirit, we will receive that gift; the Holy Spirit will come afresh into our lives when we pray. Prayer is the secret of successful evangelisation, the key that opens the treasures of heaven. Jesus shows us this by his example. He never made a big decision without turning to God his Father in prayer.

If Jesus felt it necessary to spend hours in prayer before big decisions, we too need to integrate good prayer time into every missionary activity we are engaged in. It should never be a question of getting the work done and praying when we have the time or the inclination. If we work in that way, we will quickly discover that we have less and less time and less and less inclination. We should see our time in prayer as our first act of evangelising, because only prayer evangelises our hearts.

Jesus' prayer of joy

Pope Francis wrote, "The joy of the Gospel fills the hearts and lives of all who encounter Jesus. Those who accept his offer of salvation are set free from sin, sorrow, inner emptiness and loneliness."[10] When we experience that joy of the Gospel we respond in prayer as Jesus did when he said, "I thank you Father, Lord of heaven and earth, because you have hidden these things from the wise and the intelligent and have revealed them to infants; yes, Father, for such was your gracious will" (Matthew 11:25-26).

St Paul, the greatest evangelist, shared with us the secret of his indefatigable energy as a missionary disciple when he wrote, "Pray in the Spirit at all times in every prayer and supplication" (Ephesians 6:18). Prayer should never be absent from any of our evangelising enterprises. While we pray before we go out to do the work, we try to remember that we are also speaking to Jesus as we meet people and talk with them. Jesus tells us, "just as you did it to one of the least of these who are members of my family, you did it to me" (Matthew 25:40). Jesus totally identifies himself with each person. So, we can find Jesus in every person we meet.

Christ's union with each human being

The Second Vatican Council gave us the beautiful teaching that "by His incarnation the Son of God has united Himself in some fashion with every [human being]."[11] Jesus Christ is a brother to every human being ever born into this world. Jesus is united to every person you meet and seek to evangelise and to all the millions of people who might never even think of listening to an evangelist.

---

10 Pope Francis, *Evangelii Gaudium*, 1.
11 Second Vatican Council, *Gaudium et Spes* (Pastoral Constitution on the Church in the Modern World), 22.

For this reason, the Second Vatican Council could say:

> For, since Christ died for [everyone], and since the ultimate vocation of [humankind] is in fact one, and divine, we ought to believe that the Holy Spirit in a manner known only to God offers to [everyone] the possibility of being associated with this paschal mystery.[12]

That is a most consoling teaching of the Church. It should give us great confidence as we go about our missionary tasks. People's salvation does not depend on us. Christ has redeemed them. But the knowledge and the joy of knowing their Redeemer and rejoicing in their salvation does, to a certain extent, depend on us. We have good news for them, good news that St Paul summarised when he wrote, "Jesus our Lord… was handed over to death for our trespasses and was raised for our justification" (Romans 4:24-25). It is the risen, glorified, eternal Lord Jesus who justifies and reconciles us with God the Father.

We have God's assurance that when we accept Jesus Christ as our Lord and Saviour and open our hearts to receive the Holy Spirit, all our sins are forgiven, everything in the past is made new and we can be at peace with God and with ourselves. It is not our peace; it is Christ's peace which he gives to us. As his parting gift to his disciples he said: "Peace I leave with you; my peace I give to you. I do not give to you as the world gives. Do not let your hearts be troubled, and do not let them be afraid" (John 14:27). As the Lord's missionary disciple, you will receive that peace of Christ each day.

---

12 Second Vatican Council, *Gaudium et Spes*, 22.

Personal spiritual exercise

Begin with this prayer to the Holy Spirit.

Come, Holy Spirit, fill the hearts of your faithful and enkindle in them the fire of your love. Send forth your Spirit and they shall be created. And you shall renew the face of the earth.

O God, who by the light of the Holy Spirit did instruct the hearts of the faithful, grant that by the same Holy Spirit we may be truly wise and ever enjoy his consolations. Through Christ Our Lord. Amen.

Take some time now (ten to fifteen minutes) to be still in God's presence and open your heart to receive the gift of the Holy Spirit.

- Centre yourself; sit upright, two feet firmly on the floor; breathe rhythmically with deep breaths, in and out, from the abdomen; clear your mind of all preoccupations.

- Bring yourself to bodily stillness.

- Now, hear in your heart the great prayer of St Paul: "May the God of hope fill you with all joy and peace in believing, so that you may abound in hope by the power of the Holy Spirit" (Romans 15:13).

- Quietly repeat that prayer and let it settle in your heart.

- Hope, peace and joy are what the Holy Spirit wants you to have in abundance. Open your heart to receive these gifts and thank the Holy Spirit for them.

- Now be still for some time in the presence of God as you welcome the Holy Spirit into your heart.

- As you are about to finish your time of prayer, focus again on your breathing while you relax in God's presence.

- Bring yourself gently back to your daily concerns.

This spiritual exercise will deepen your awareness of the presence of the Holy Spirit in your heart and enable you to live by those gifts of hope, joy and peace.

Other titles by Jim McManus C.Ss.R.
available from Redemptorist Publications

www.rpbooks.co.uk

The Healing Power of the Sacraments

Healing in the Spirit

Hallowed Be Thy Name

All Generations Will Call Me Blessed

The Inside Job: a spirituality of true self-esteem

I Am My Body: Blessed John Paul's theology of the body

Finding Forgiveness: personal and spiritual perspectives
(with Dr Stephanie Thornton)

Searching for Serenity: spirituality in later life
(with Dr Stephanie Thornton)

Going to Mass: becoming the Eucharist we celebrate

Fountain of Grace: celebrating 150 years of the Icon of Love

Embraced by Mercy: God's ultimate gift

At Home in the Mysteries of Christ: the grace of the Rosary

Our Spiritual Lifeline: the oxygen of Christian prayer

Sent to Proclaim the Gospel: honouring the legacy of St Paul VI